Illuminations from the Soul

Soul

The beauty and wonder of nature's light and its poetic inspiration

Lisa K Nelson

Forward

There is beauty all around us. Whether found in the light of day or the shadows of night, there lives a captivating beauty called nature. She escapes many even though she is as close as the breath from our lips.

We traverse our days sleep-walking, oblivious to the gifts and wonders around us. Igno- rant of the peace visual beauty can bring. Yet all we need to do is awaken and walk through our days with eyes wide open and enjoy what we have been blessed with.

I've been fascinated with light and how it creates living art since I was very little. I recall when I was five I rode in the back seat of our family car on our way to Grandma's house. It was autumn and the leaves in Minnesota were changing color. As we approached a stop sign and slowed, I noticed a brilliantly colored ruby leaf waving in the breeze at the top of one of the elms that lined the street. I suddenly realized I was the only one in the whole world to have witnessed that beautiful leaf shimmering at that very moment. I was in awe. Perhaps it was a strange thing for a kid to think about at that age but that memory and the lesson I learned from that has stayed with me through the years. My motto now as an adult is to live for today, capture every joyful beautiful moment that you can. We are only here for a short measure so take nothing for granted and LIVE with your eyes Wide-Open!

I hope you enjoy my photos of light which I have chosen for this first book. I've used those which inspired me to write poetry, another of my creative outlets.

Dedication

Life... a journey made up of many paths. One is not necessarily better than another. We all choose our way every day, make choices that lead us to the next step along our way. The hope is to make positive choices that will propel us into positive circumstances and opportunities. For some, the beginning of life began with loving caring people who taught us and guided us in learning how to make decisions that would benefit us as well as others. I am fortunate to be one of those people. My parents are the most precious gift I could ever have wished for. They have seen me through many tough times and health challenges, and they have stuck with me as I set out to find my way again at the age of 50. It is only fitting that I dedicate this first book to them, Janet and Sherman Nelson. My heart is full because of them.

Chapter 1: Morning Light

"Oh spirit of the wind, teach me and guide me that I might learn and know the truth."
-Lisa KNelson

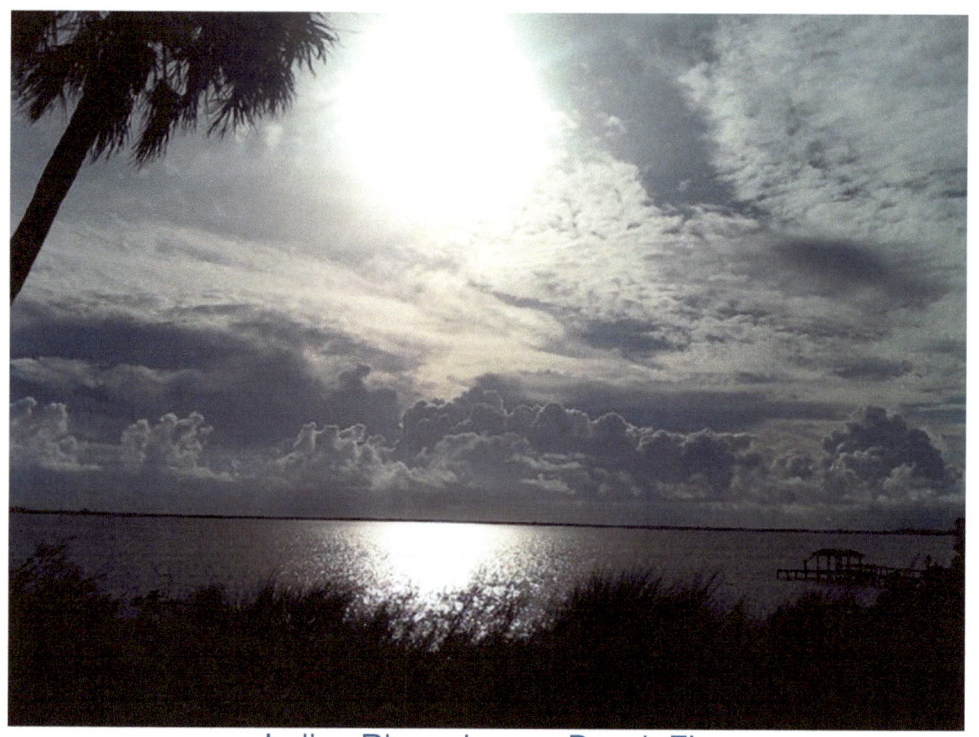

Indian River, Jensen Beach FL

Awaken

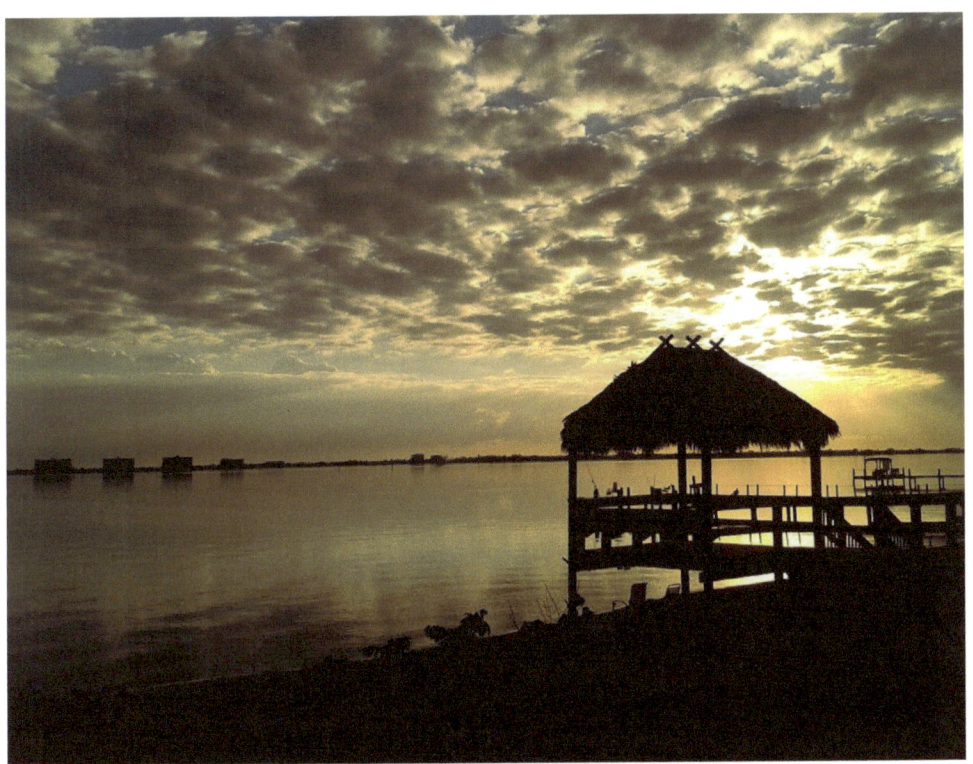

Indian River, Jensen Beach FL

Quietly comes the dawn,
with swift arms it embraces us,
with silent breath it bathes us,
giving life to color.

Ocean's Breath

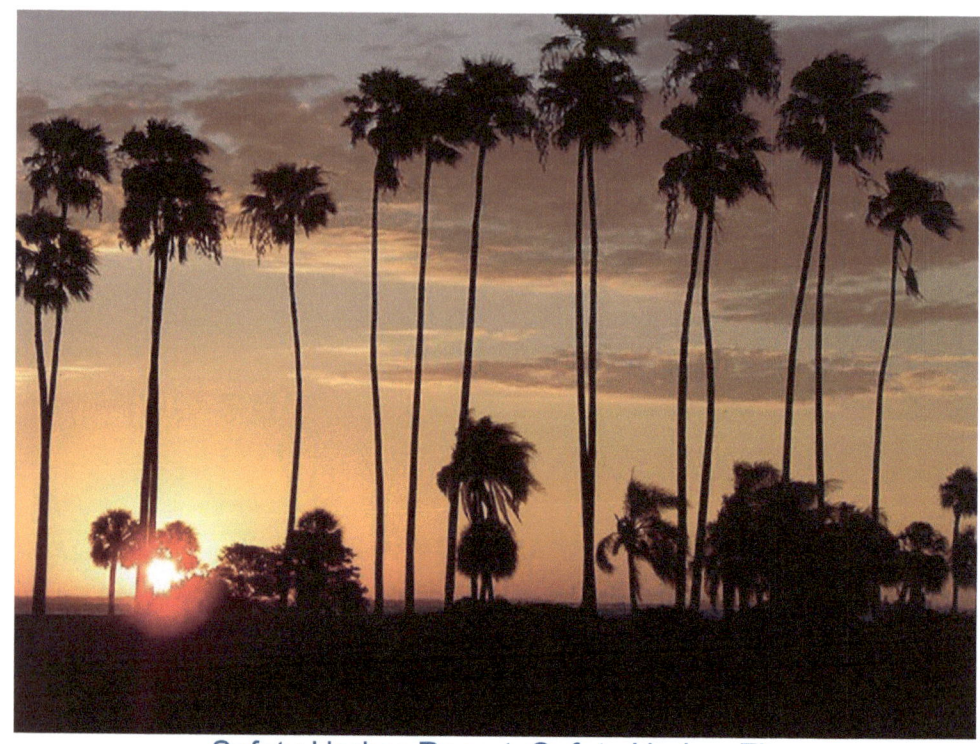

Safety Harbor Resort, Safety Harbor FL

Warm soft winds caress my cheek
I smell that salty spray
I eagerly go outside to greet
the beginning of my day.

Dawn's Light

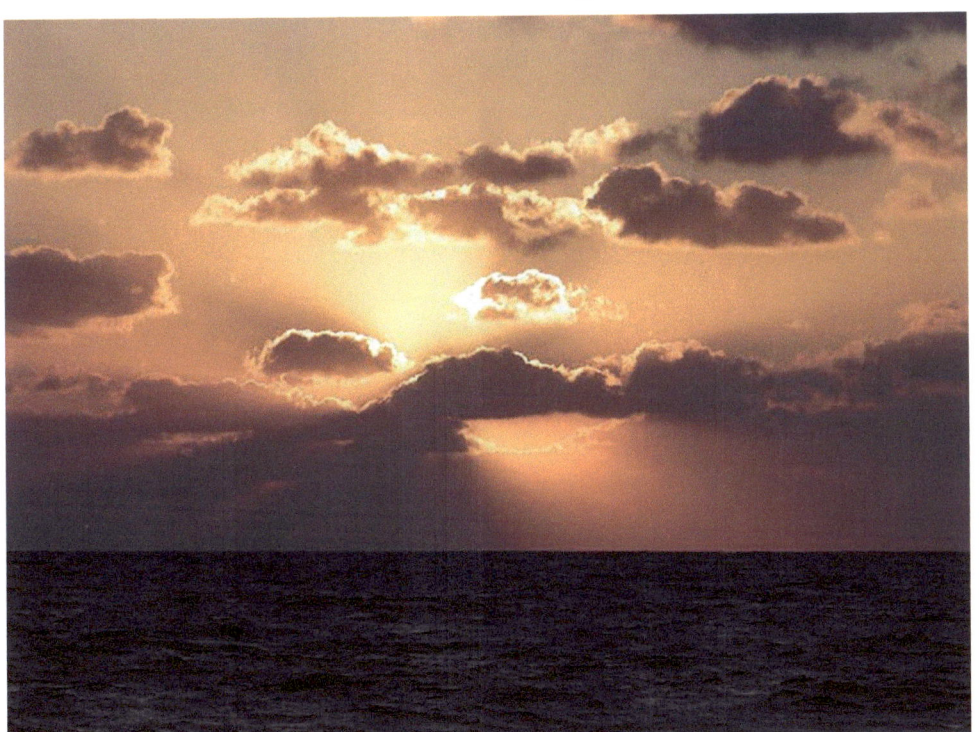

Vero Beach FL

Silently my heart beats,
it soars past the stars,
it penetrates the darkness,
it finds solace in the light,
the sweet dawning light.

Good Morning Sunshine

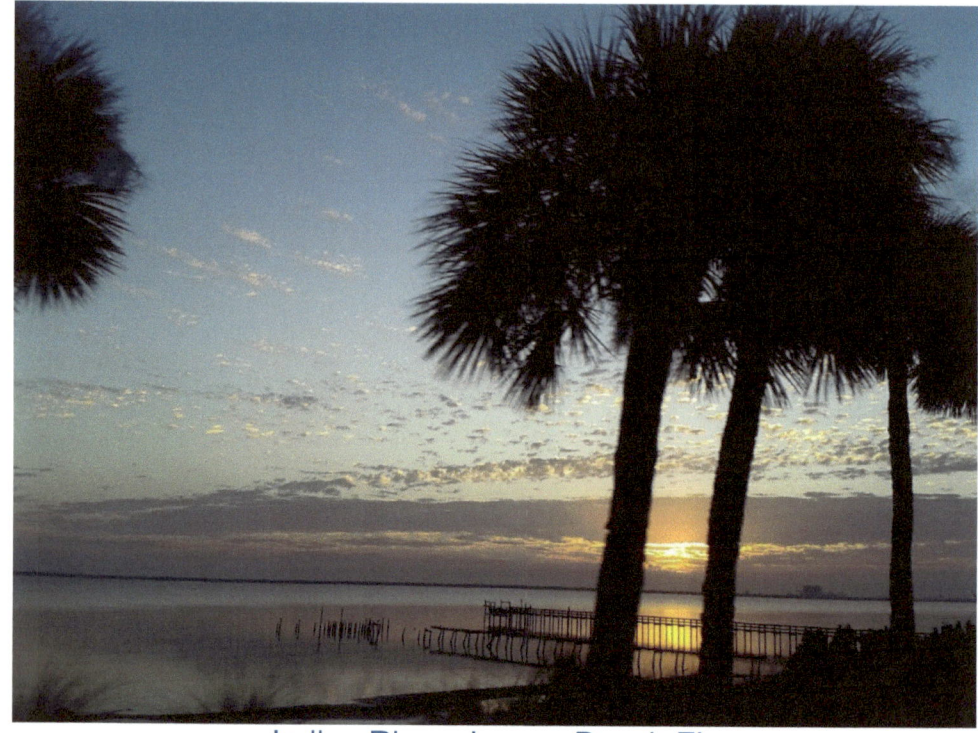

Indian River, Jensen Beach FL

The morning sun lifts up his head,
as clouds drift by above
he wakens, looking east then west,
giving Night a gentle nudge
He shines upon all he purveys,
as far as he can see
his robe of light encircles all,
with life and energy.

Will-O-Wisps

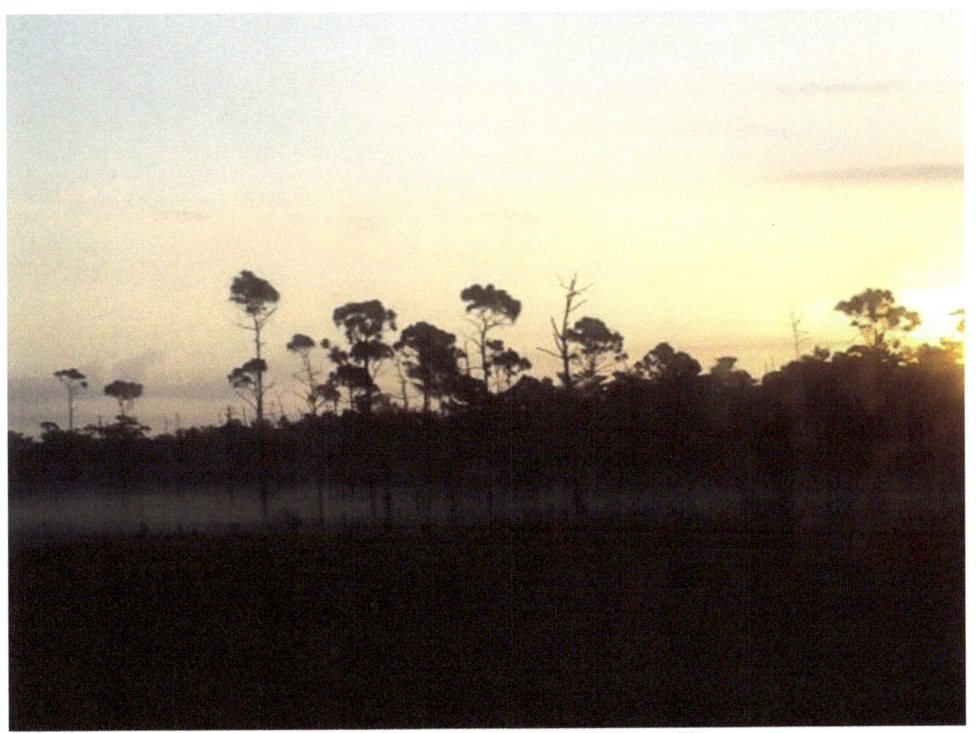

I-95 close to Daytona Beach FL

Wisps of wind, ghostly light,
drift slowly by, into day from night
Puffs of smoke leave morning dew
giving drink to grass and animals too.

Ocean's Waters

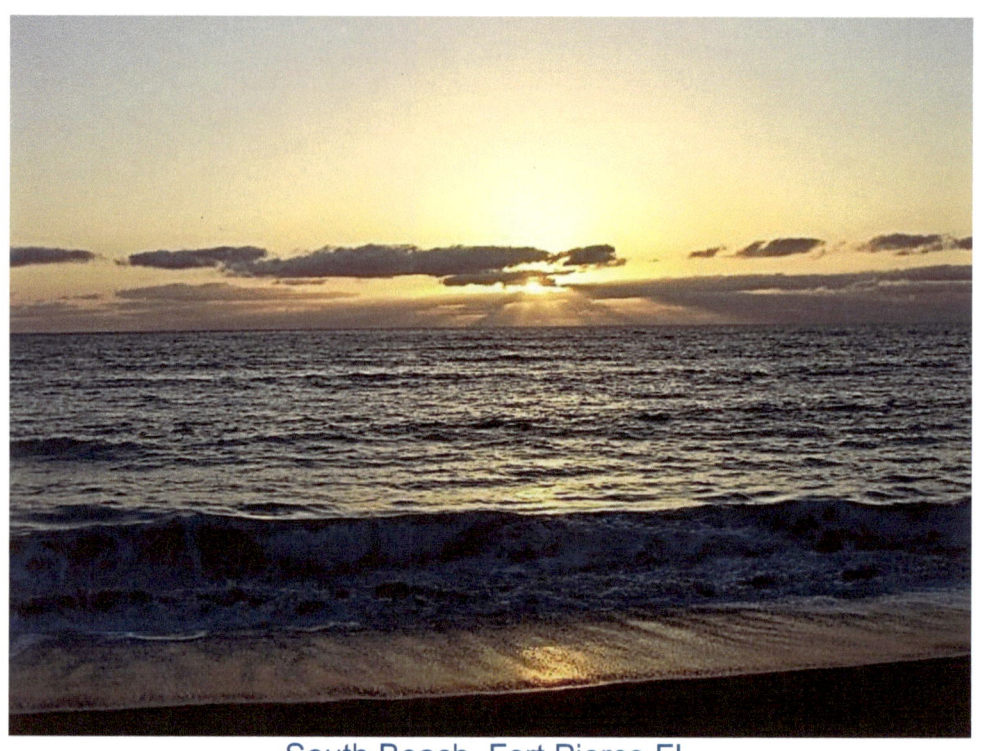

South Beach, Fort Pierce FL

Mesmerizing
Tranquilizing
Calming waters in the midst of turmoil
Churning waters in the midst of peace

Chapter 2: Day Light

"Those who remain unmoved by the wind of joy silently follow the Path." --Bodhidharma

South Beach, Fort Pierce FL

Soaking Up The Sun

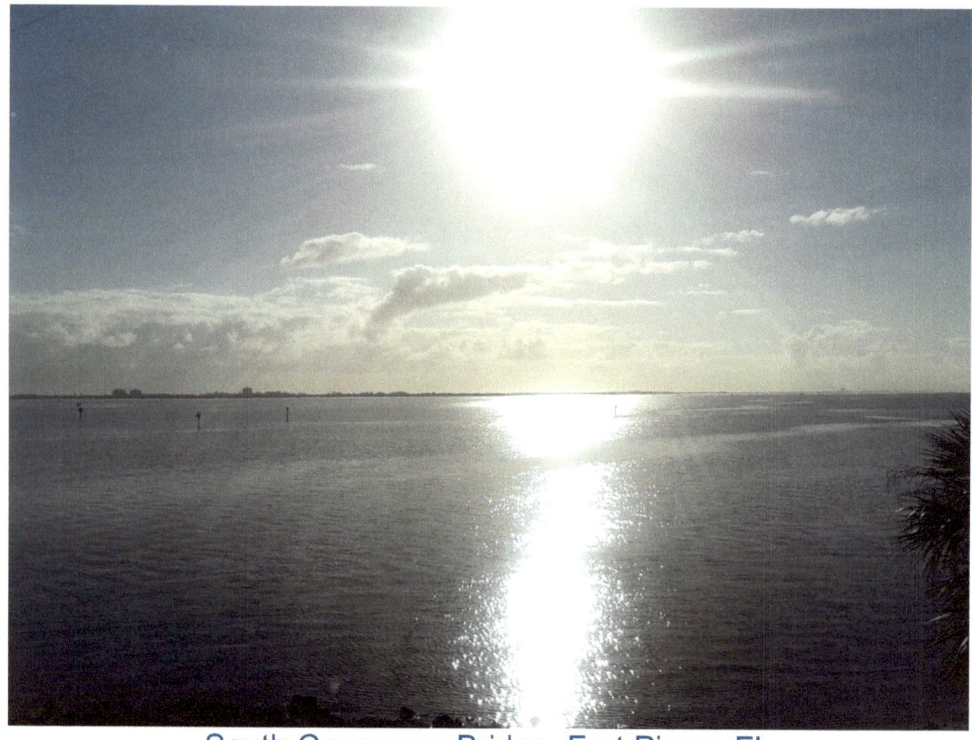

South Causeway Bridge, Fort Pierce FL

Bright and glorious light
Your brilliance astounds me
Your warmth surrounds me
Where the light is, there is no darkness.

Waiting

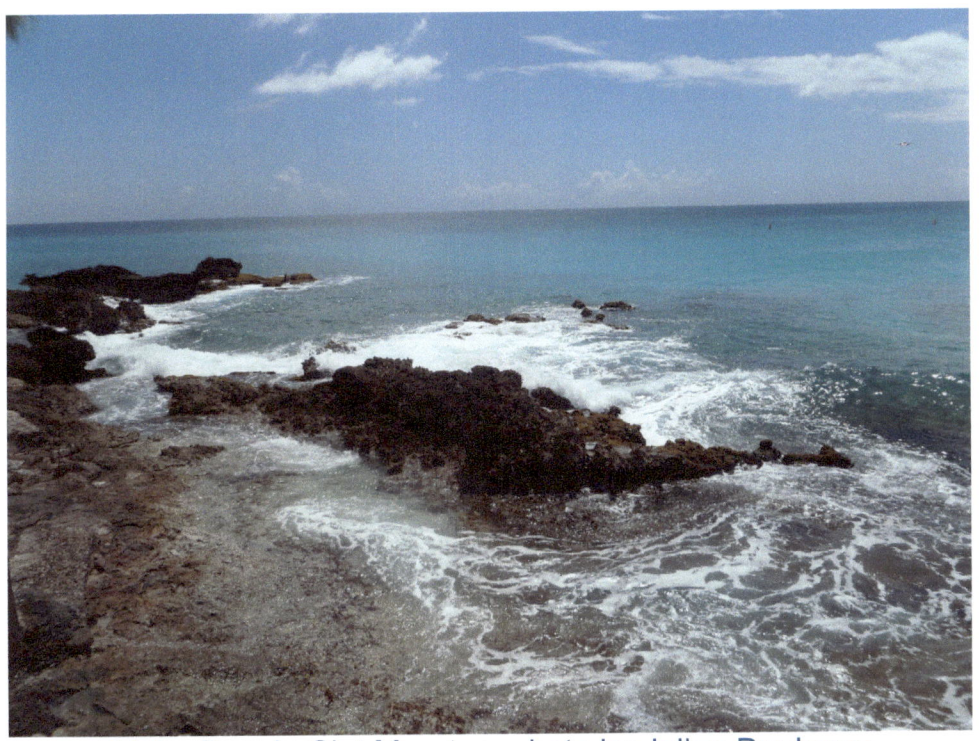

Maho Beach, Sint Maarten; photo by Julian Dunleavy

Times of challenge,
times of change
words may fail me,
vision strange
hardship, pressures,
limbo still waiting, anxious,
I've had my fill.
But truth persists,
all answers wait,
delivered on that perfect date,
as time so often has a way
of showing up, it's not too late.
Divinely guided, directions new
He never fails us, you know that too.

Breathe

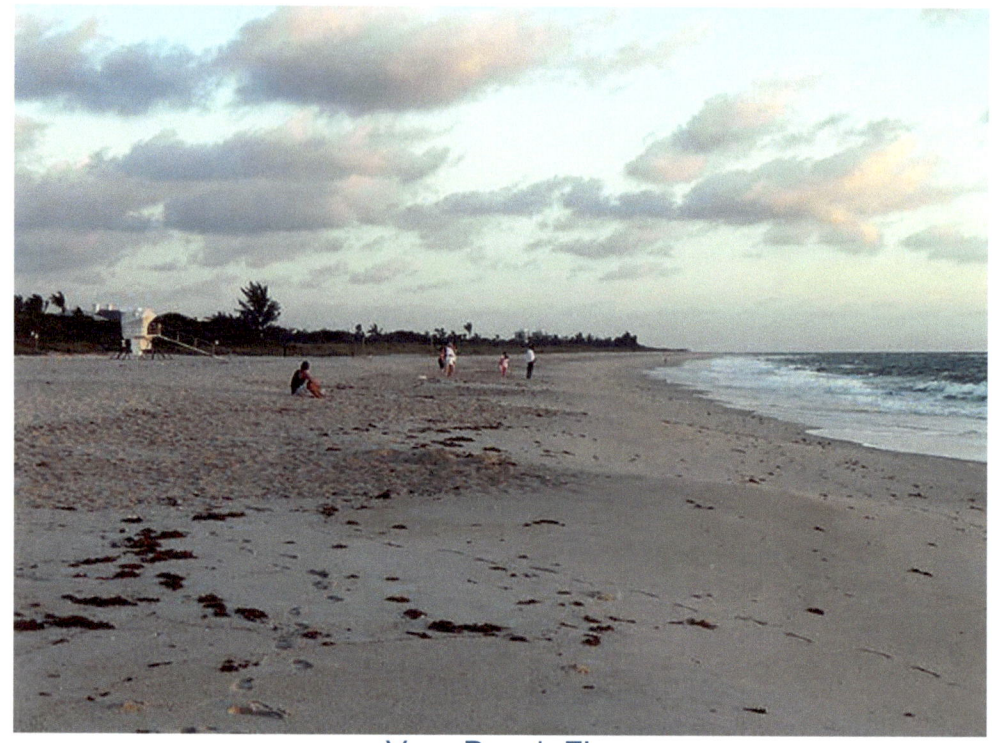

Vero Beach FL

Capture moments now at hand
breathe in deeply as you can
let it not just pass you by
live it, feel it, don't ask why
Our time is precious, that is true.
so spend it wisely on what you do
examine closely, "happiness"
if its missing, there's the test;
Admit what's lacking in your life
make the effort, end your strife
once you've altered patterns old,
your life now priceless, fine as gold.

Roar of the Lion

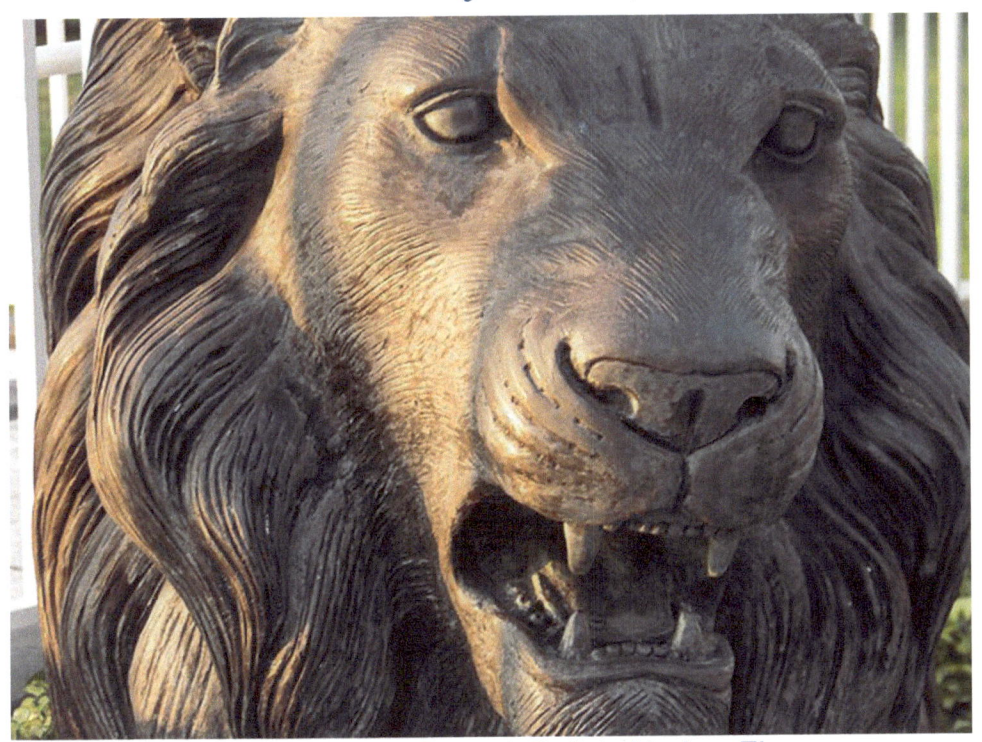

Safety Harbor Resort, Safety Harbor FL

The golden sun sits upon his brow
he's silent, starring, alive somehow
this proud guardian standing straight
he's thwarting danger from these gates.

Serenity

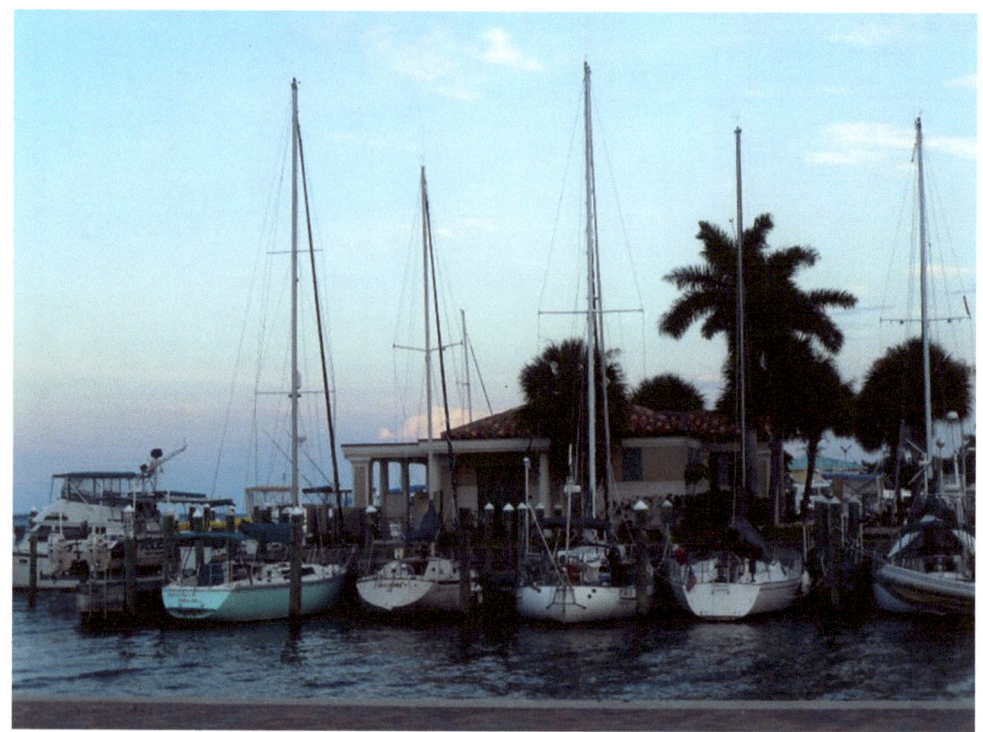

Fort Pierce Marina, Fort Pierce FL

Peaceful rocking of the boat
swaying gently as it floats
Moored upon the water deep
it lulls me into drifting sleep

Dance with Joy

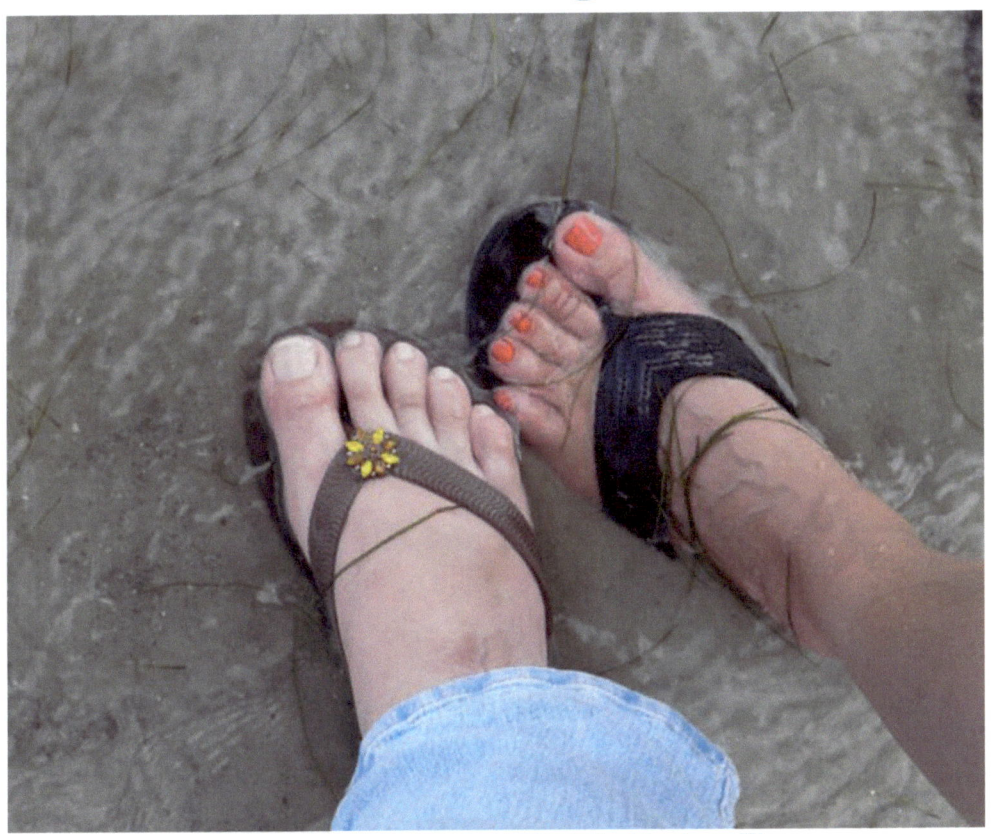

Safety Harbor Resort, Safety Harbor FL

My feet were made for dancing with joy,
not tip-toeing through life.
So when it comes time to remove my shoes
at the end of life's journey,
I want the soles to be worn,
the threads to be bare,
and the heels to be missing

Chapter 3: Evening Light

"If we have no peace, it is because we have forgotten that we belong to each other."
-Mother Teresa

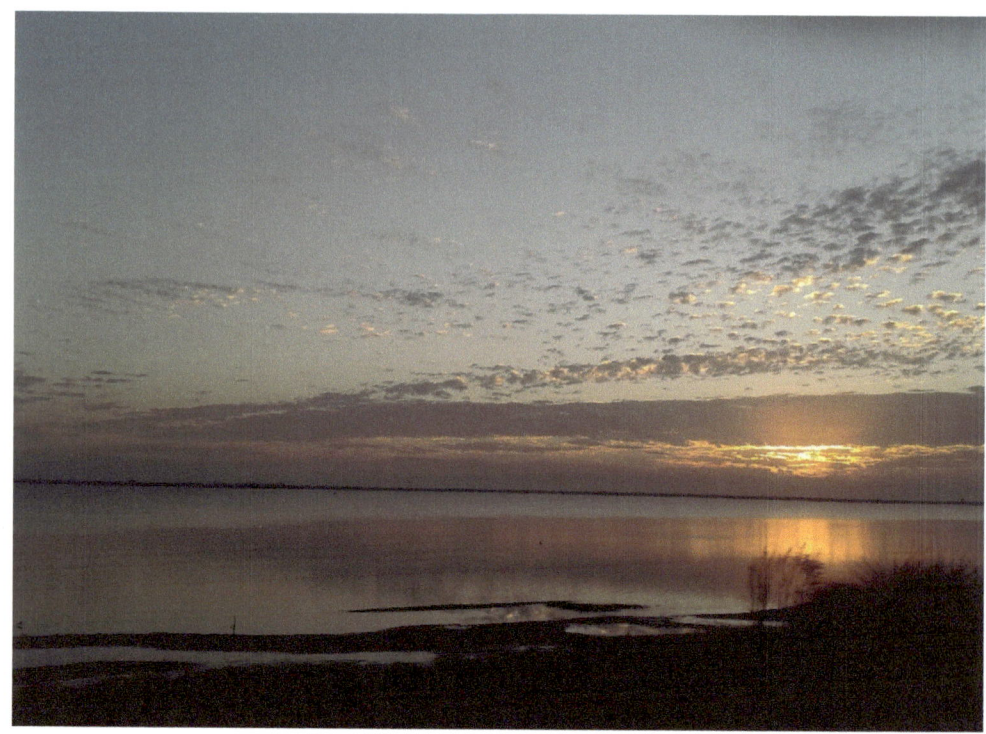

Indian River, Jensen Beach FL

Natural Wonder

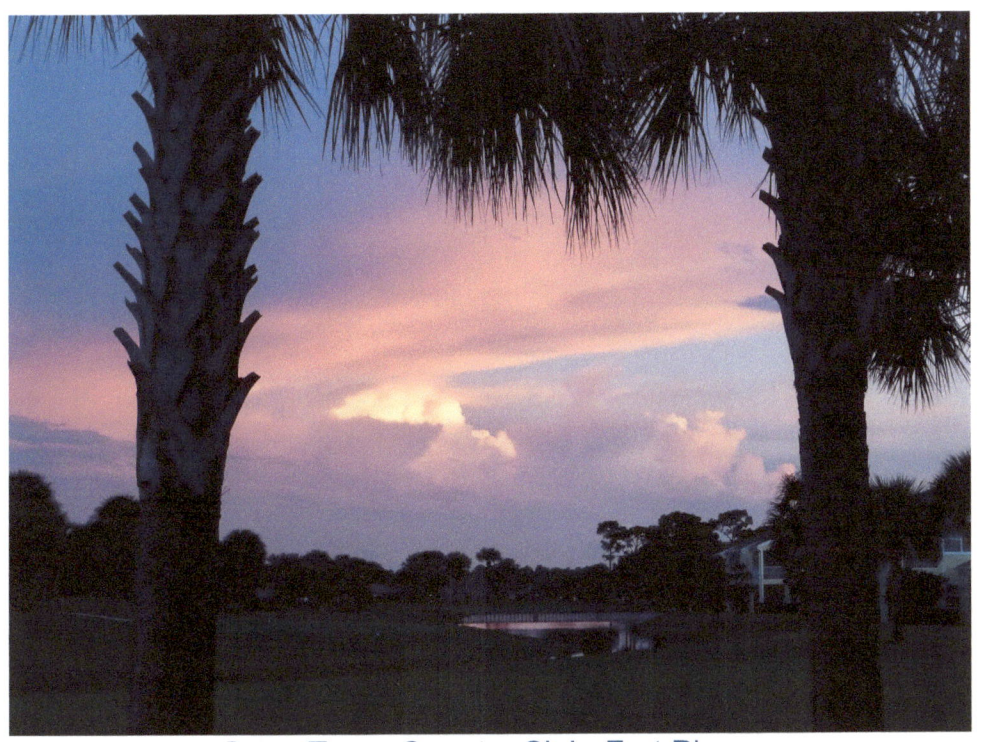

Gator Trace Country Club, Fort Pierce

Nature bends to no man's demands.
It is ever present, ever changing,
and always in control.
Its gift is beauty, its reward is peace.
Take note and breathe it in fully,
for living in cadence with nature
will enrich us, restore us, and
renew us in body, mind, and spirit.

The Meadow

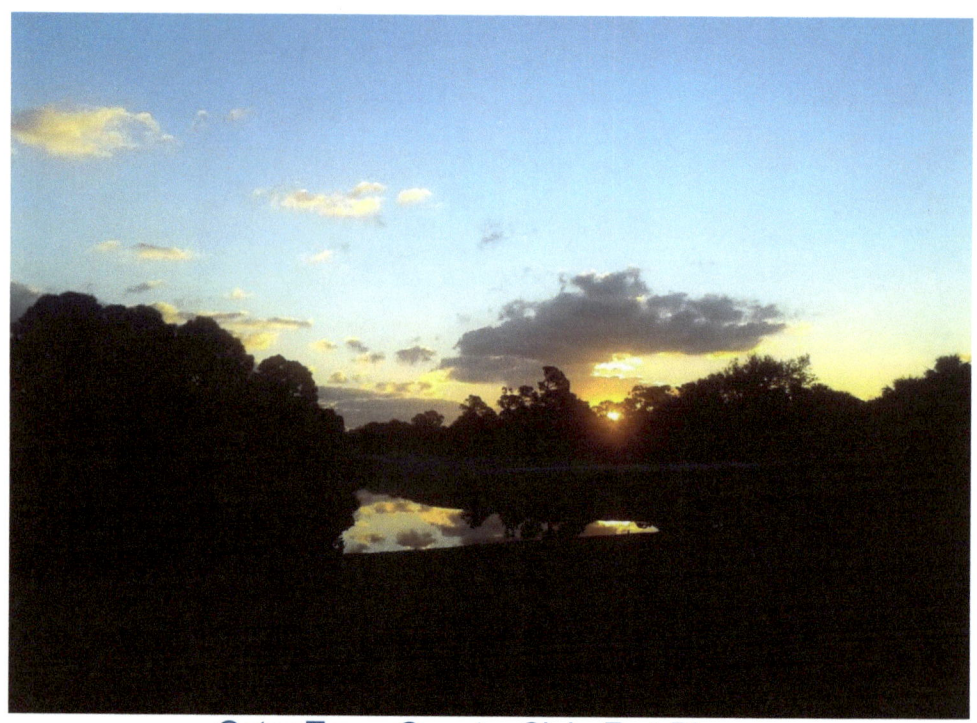

Gator Trace Country Club, Fort Pierce

The sun gently sets on the meadow,
mirrored colors reflect in the sky
The stillness is broken by echo
of cranes calling others nearby.
Calm water paints pictures above us,
lends colors that may just astound
it leaves us breathless in waiting to see
new wonders of sight and of sound.

New Horizons

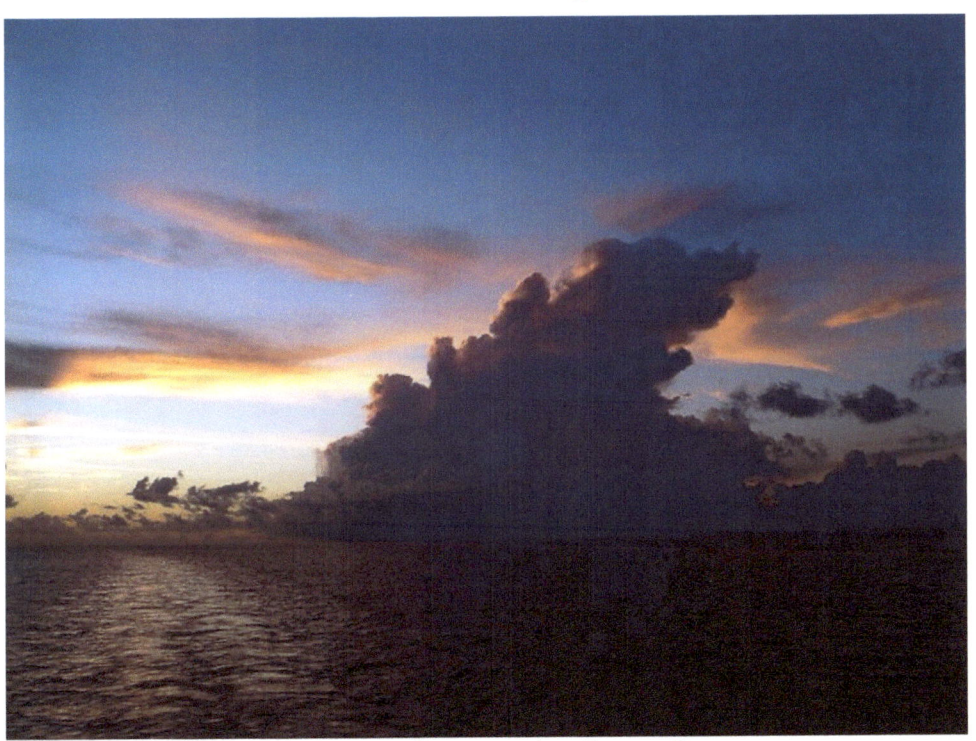

Caribbean Sunset, the Open Sea

Goodbye to yesterdays,
we're leaving you behind.
There are new suns to see,
new light to receive,
new thoughts to perceive
and new dreams to achieve.
We've loved you and we always will,
but it is time to embrace our new future,
a new beginning,
and step forward into that light.

Skies on Fire

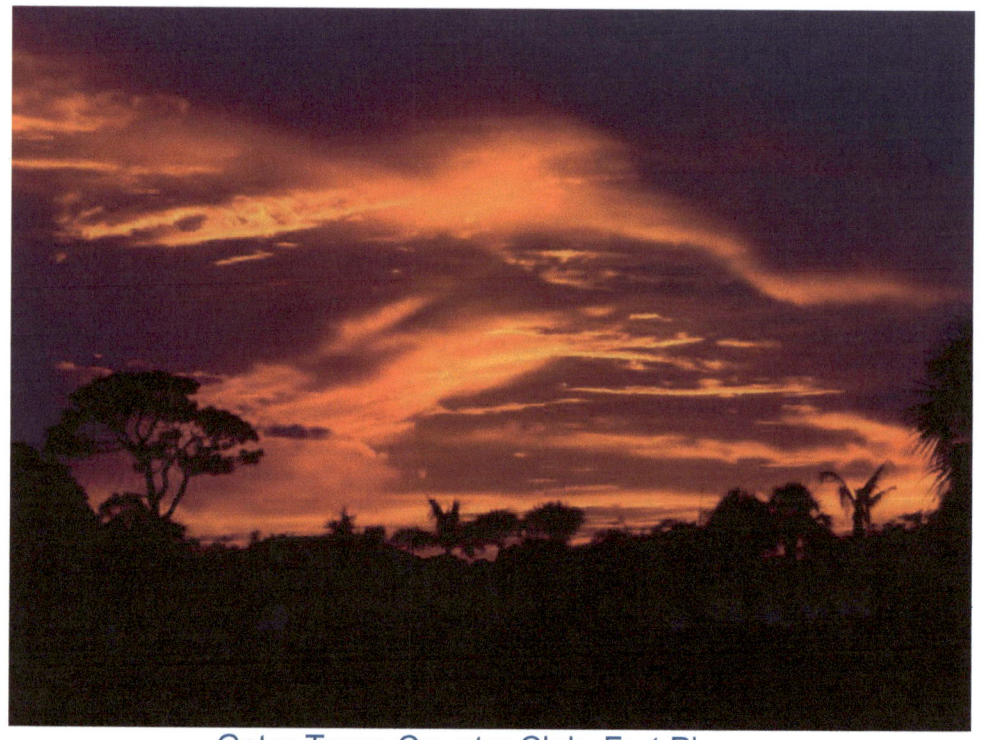

Gator Trace Country Club, Fort Pierce

Molten colors, swirling clouds
paints a picture, an evening shroud.
Purples, pinks and yellows too
an artist palette, orange-red hue.
Makes me grateful for my sight,
I'm blessed I stepped outside tonight.

Guiding Light

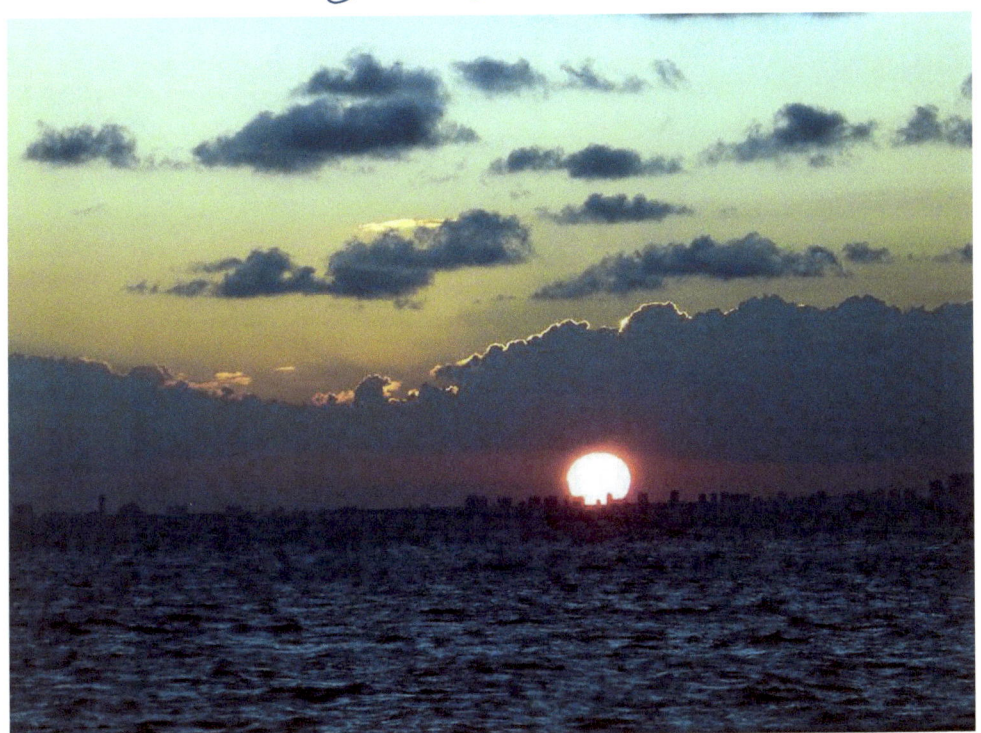

Sunset over Miami FL

Guiding light, you've done your work.
It's time to put out your flame.
With rest and sleep you'll be refreshed,
ready to guide us again.

Dreams & Visions

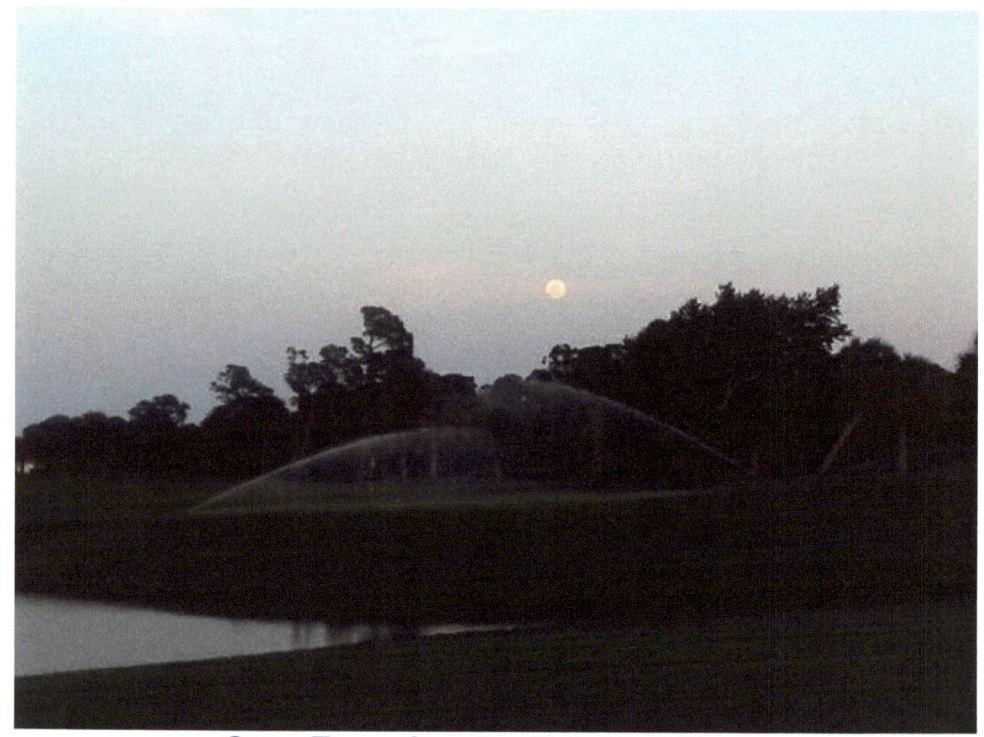

Gator Trace Country Club, Fort Pierce

The vision never fades,
the promise never fails,
a dream is only crushed
when believing in false tales.
So listen not to people
who say it can't be done,
Just put your mind & heart at ease
and have a bit of fun.
Step by step you'll make it
before you know it's through,
you'll have that dream you dreamt of
right there in front of you.

Celestial Moon

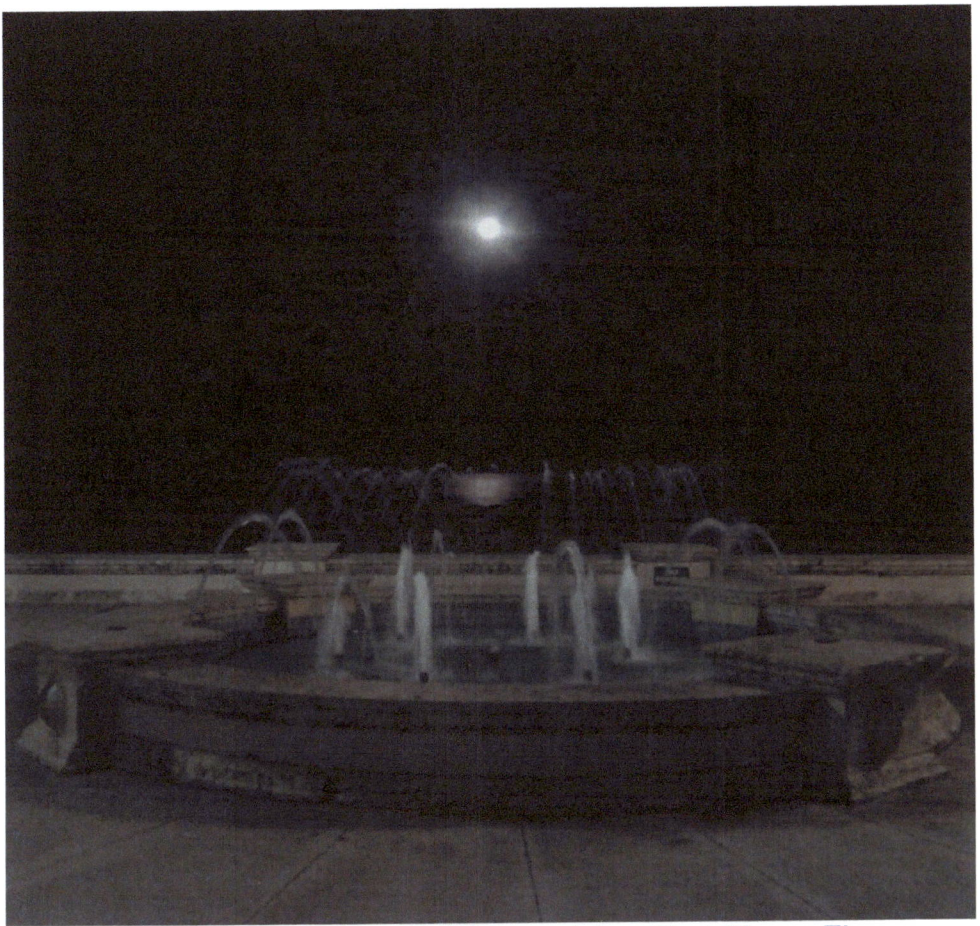

Fort Pierce Marina - Full Moon rising, Fort Pierce FL

Celestial moon, sister of the sun,
Carries on with the Day's deeds;
Lighting the way for night travelers;
Extending her hand to illuminate the darkness;
Painting the landscape with shadows and highlights;
Restoring sight to those blinded by night.
Let Nature drink in her beauty
and the waters reflect her lovely countenance.

Moon Fairy

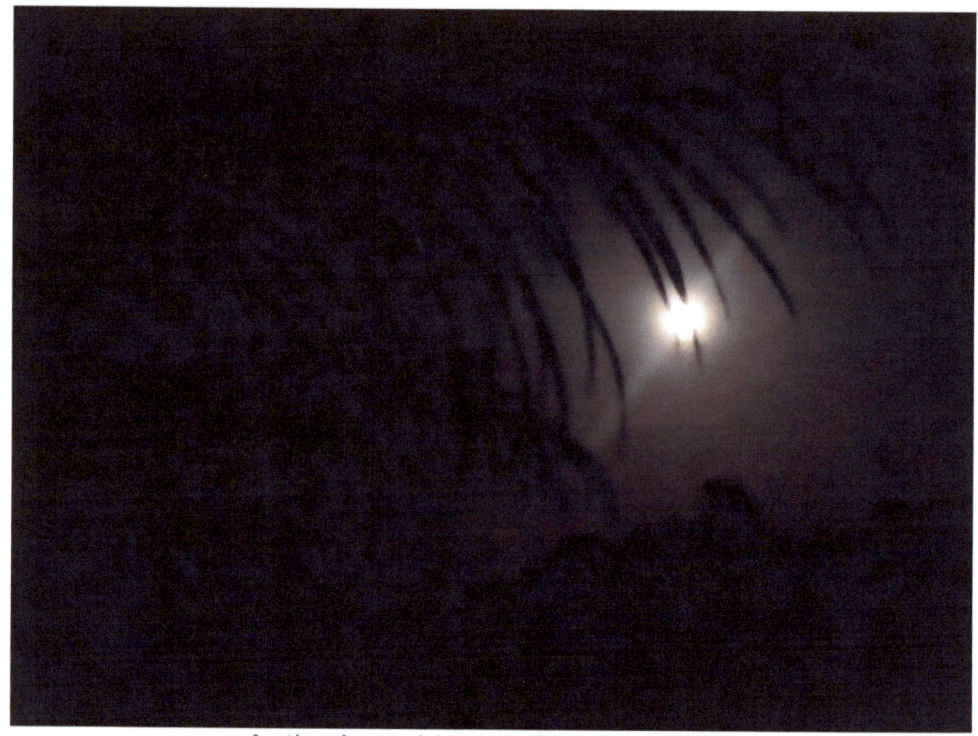

Author's residence, Fort Pierce FL

Is this a fairy upon my tree,
is she dancing there for me?
I see her through my window bright,
a shining diamond in the night.

About the Author

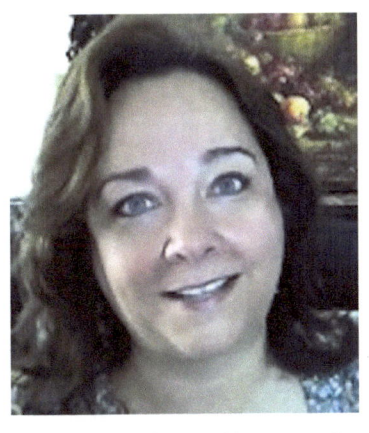

Lisa Nelson grew up on the east coast of Florida and survived bone cancer from an early age. That experience drew her into medicine and she became educated as a clinical microbiologist and then as a board certified Physician Assistant. Later in life she worked as an elder-care giver and assisted in wound care of diabetics and cancer patients. All these life experiences molded her outlook in a positive way and gave her a purpose of encouraging and uplifting others. Since art has been a very large part of her life, she decided she could share her positive energy with a larger population through her love of writing, photography and jewelry design.

It is Lisa's belief that creative expression is important in maintaining balance and fostering happiness. She has been involved in artistic ventures throughout her life and she also has a rich family history of members who were and are artists and artisans. Most notably was a 20th century color pen & ink artist by the name of Fred Lexow who became quite famous for his nature paintings, hand carved duck decoys, and hand-painted fishing lures.

"It is my hope that this book touches people in a positive uplifting way which leaves them feeling good after having read it. Enjoy!" ~Lisa Nelson